306
REY

DEMCO

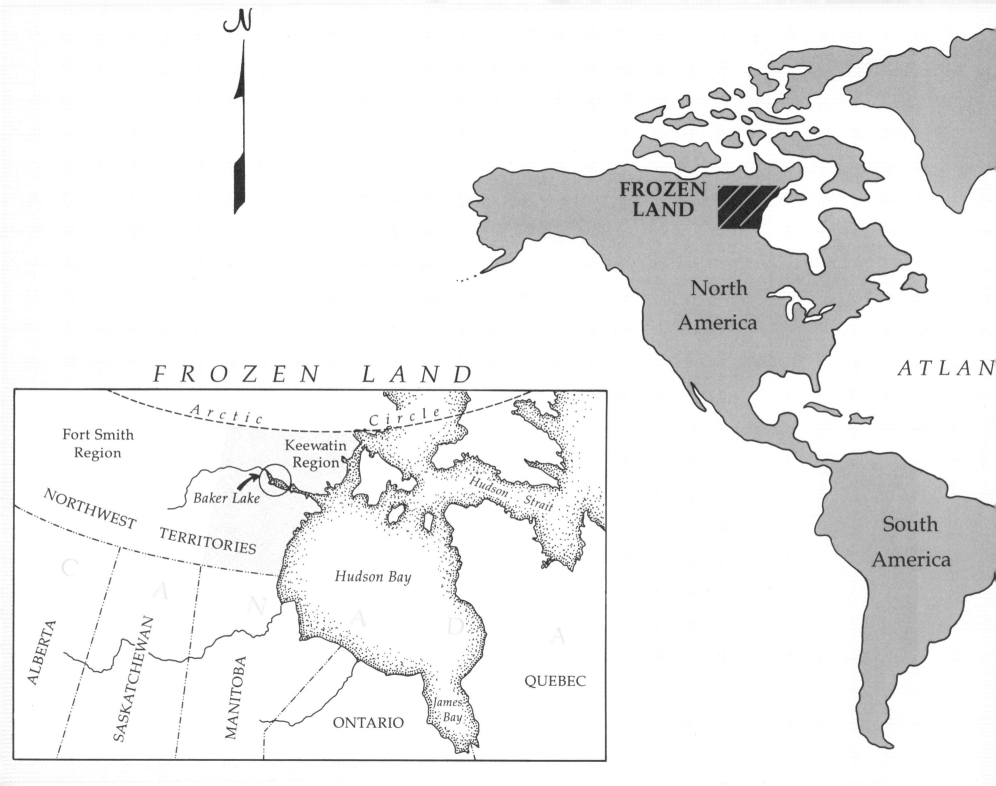

N

FROZEN
LAND

North
America

ATLAN

South
America

FROZEN LAND

Arctic Circle

Fort Smith
Region

Keewatin
Region

Baker Lake

Hudson Strait

NORTHWEST

TERRITORIES

Hudson Bay

C   A   N   A   D   A

ALBERTA

SASKATCHEWAN

MANITOBA

QUEBEC

James
Bay

ONTARIO

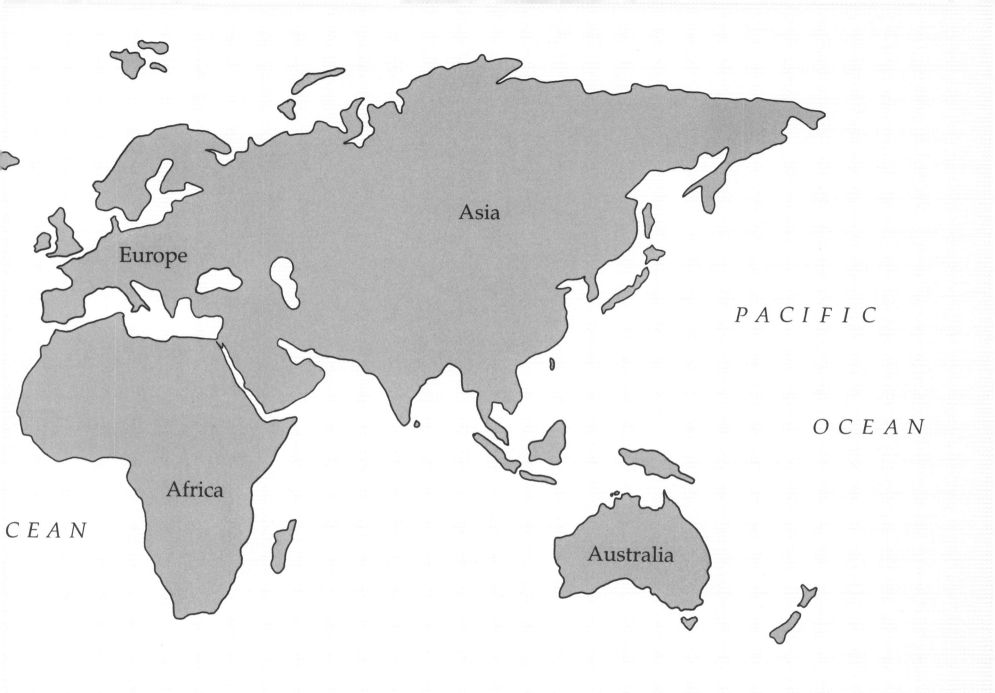

FROZEN LAND
VANISHING CULTURES
Jan Reynolds

Harcourt Brace & Company

San Diego   New York   London

Requests for permission to make copies of any part of
the work should be mailed to: Permissions Department,
Harcourt Brace & Company, 6277 Sea Harbor Drive,
Orlando, Florida 32887-6777.

Library of Congress Cataloging-in-Publication Data
Reynolds, Jan, 1956–
Frozen land: vanishing cultures/Jan Reynolds. — 1st ed.
p.   cm.
Summary: Describes the traditional ways of life of an
Inuit family living in the Canadian Northwest Territories
and some of the changes they have had to face.
ISBN 0-15-238787-0 (hc.) — ISBN 0-15-238788-9 (pbk.)
1. Eskimos — Northwest Territories — Baker Lake.
(Lake — Social life and customs — Juvenile literature.)
2. Baker Lake (N.W.T.: Lake) — Social life and
customs — Juvenile literature.   [1. Eskimos — Northwest
Territories.]   I. Title.
E99.E7R44   1993
306′.089′97107194–dc20   92-30324

B C D E F   B C D E F (pbk.)

Printed in Singapore

*To my generous friends
and to all friendships
around the world
—J. R.*

*To take the photographs in this book, the author used two
35mm cameras with 20mm, 35mm, 105mm, and 180mm lenses.
The display type and text type were set in Palatino by the
Photocomposition Center, Harcourt Brace & Company,
San Diego, California.
Color separations were made by Bright Arts, Ltd., Singapore.
Printed and bound by Tien Wah Press, Singapore
Production supervision by Warren Wallerstein and Ginger Boyer
Designed by Camilla Filancia*

The Inuit known as the caribou hunters live near the shores of Qamanituaq, an inlet of Hudson Bay. Throughout most of the year, their land is covered with snow. When these people travel and hunt along the frozen shores and across the windy plains, they live in igloos, round houses made out of blocks of snow. When the ice breaks up and melts for a short time in the warmer months, they live in tents made of caribou hide. Long ago, they depended on the caribou for survival and waited for their annual migration to hunt them.

But this ancient way of life is disappearing. When fur traders and trappers from Europe came to the lands of the Inuit, the caribou herds became smaller and moved away. Without the regular migration of the caribou, Inuit life changed.

Because the Inuit believe that they, the caribou, and all nature share a common spirit, they respect the land and the animals, depending on them to provide what is necessary for a good life. We are all part of the same human family, and we all depend on the land and nature to provide us with the things we need to live. Perhaps we can learn from the relationship the Inuit have with their natural surroundings before their way of life vanishes forever.

As the sun sets on the edge of the frozen shores of Qamanituaq, a large inlet of Hudson Bay, Kenalogak asks her grandmother for one more story.

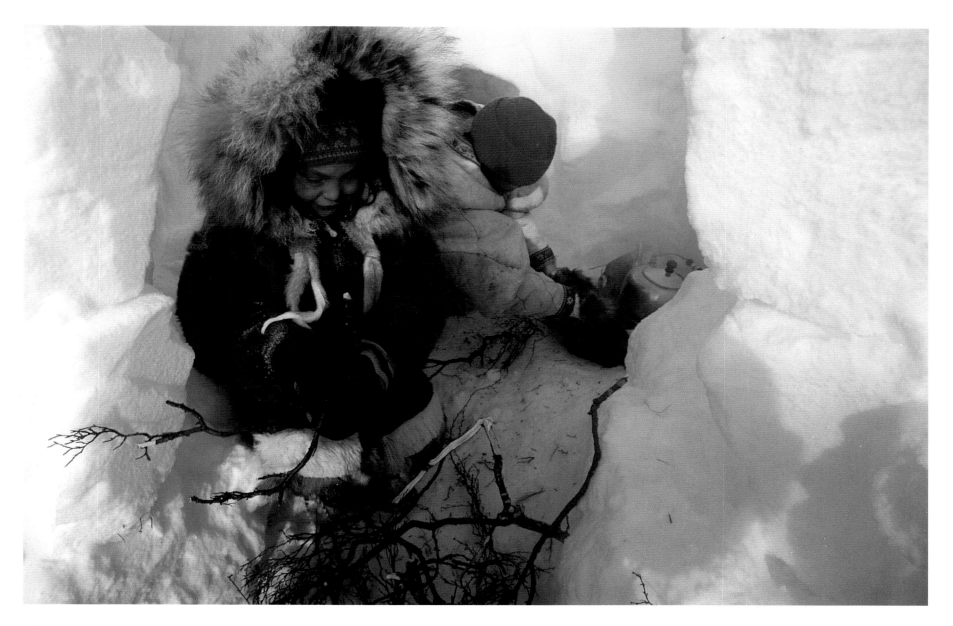

They hurry to prepare tea before the chill of darkness comes, and Kenalogak's grandmother begins her tale.

"Long ago your grandfather traveled great distances with his dogs and sled in search of the caribou herd. As Inuit, we depend on *tuktu*, the caribou, to provide us with meat to eat and skin to make warm clothing."

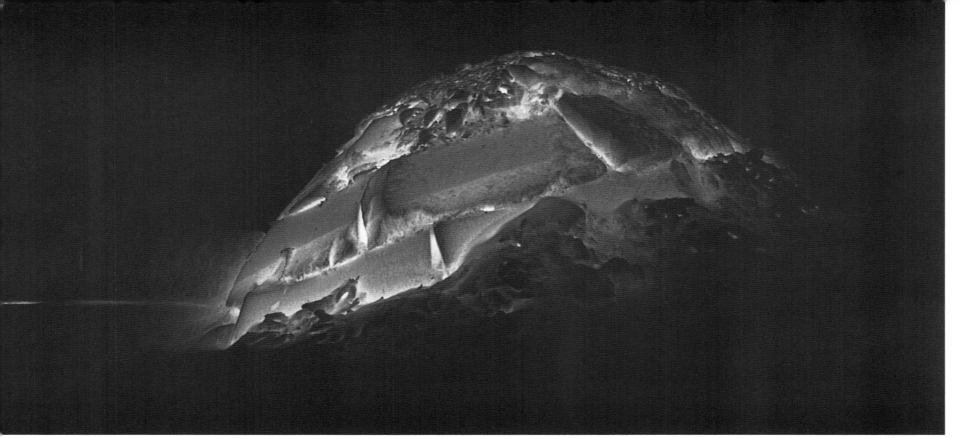

Igloo at night

"To protect himself from the winds on the open plains, your grandfather would build an igloo out of blocks of snow."

Grandmother's tale goes on into the night. When Kenalogak falls asleep, she dreams of a long sled journey over the snow-covered land.

High winds cause ridges in the snow and ice.

The next day, the cold winds that often blow across the ice are calm. Kenalogak's mother decides it is a good time to teach her daughter to fish.

Mother keeps *paniq*, little sister, warm inside her large parka while she shows Kenalogak how to move the hook up and down in the water to attract fish. Many big fish have been caught here, and they hope to catch more.

Aretak, Kenalogak's older brother, fishes on his own, behind a small windbreak of snow. He breaks a hole in the ice with a long pole, then scoops the broken ice out with a large spoonlike shovel.

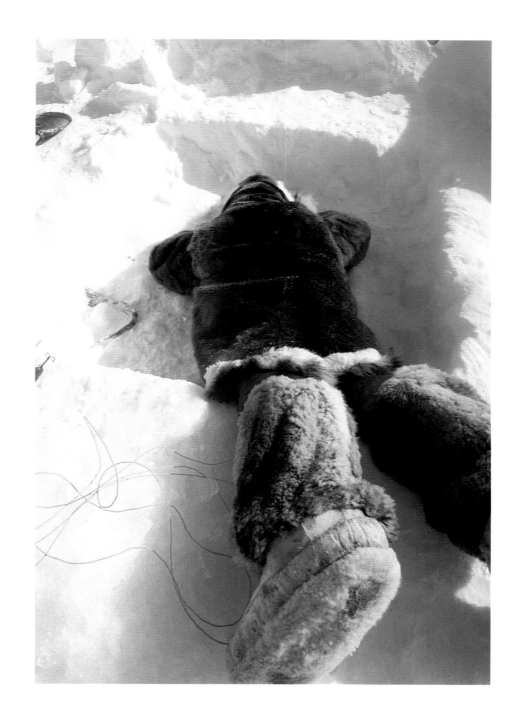

After he removes the freezing slush, Aretak lies in the snow and peers down into the hole. He is looking for a shadow or movement that could be a fish.

Kenalogak loves the taste of fresh, raw fish—it's a treat. But tuktu, the caribou, is the animal her people have depended on for their way of life. Caribou meat is the most common meal and it too is often eaten raw.

When there is plenty of caribou meat, some is left out on the snow to dry naturally. The dried meat will be eaten later when the caribou herds cannot be found. The caribou's skin is used to make clothing, blankets, and the tents the Inuit live in during the warmer months. Even the bones and antlers are made into tools the Inuit need.

When they hunt caribou, the Inuit build *inuksuk,* rock piles that are stacked to look like men. The caribou think the inuksuk are hunters, and they move away from the rock statues, unknowingly moving toward the real Inuit hunters who are waiting for them.

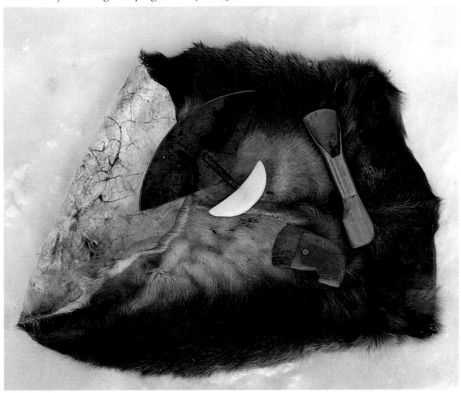

When the caribou's skin is removed, the inside is scraped clean with the curved blade of the *ulu,* a half-moon–shaped knife. After the skin has dried, it is cleaned again and softened by scraping it with a dull scooped blade.

Once the skins are soft and clean, they are ready for Mother to cut and sew into boots, pants, and parkas for the entire family.

Ptarmigan and hare also live near the frozen shores. In the winter their feathers and fur turn white so they blend into the snowy landscape. This makes them difficult to find for Inuit hunters and other predators.

Great polar bears leave tracks on the edge of the ice by the big bay where they search for seals to eat. Foxes often follow the bears so they can eat what the bears leave behind.

In this land of snow, animals need one another to live. The Inuit believe there is a life spirit in all things. This spirit connects them to their land and everything living there: the animals, birds, fish, and even the rocks and the wind share the life spirit with the Inuit.

Fox tracks inside polar bear tracks

Wolves also roam the cold, windy plain. Aretak teases his sister by covering himself in a wolf skin his father brought home from his last hunting trip.

When Kenalogak is not looking, Aretak pops up from behind the snow disguised as a wolf. Kenalogak runs until she hears her brother laughing at her. She also laughs at how silly he looks under the wolf skin.

Playing outside together on the vast frozen plain, Kenalogak and Aretak often invent their own games.

Kenalogak likes to make angels in the snow, and Aretak practices flips while they wait for their father to return.

Father has been running his dogs over the snow and ice. He is training them to work together as a team when they pull the sled.

The dogs are fast and strong. When Kenalogak's father arrives home, she helps him untie the dogs from the sled and give them food and water.

After the dogs have been taken care of, it is time to make a new igloo. Grandmother and Grandfather want a special place for the family to sing their old songs and to dance.

Kenalogak's father shows her how to shave the snow off an ice block as he teaches her how to build an igloo. While he stacks the blocks, Mother and Aretak shovel loose snow onto the sides of the igloo. This closes up the small spaces between the blocks and keeps the wind out.

While Father continues to stack the blocks, Mother builds a small entry room for the igloo. She cuts blocks out of the floor area to use for the walls. In the entry room a fire can be lit, and the smoke can escape through a small hole she will cut in the ceiling.

The most difficult part of building the igloo is closing in the roof. When cut, the edges of the blocks must be angled to fit together and support each other. It only takes about an hour for the family working together to build the igloo.

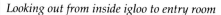
Looking out from inside igloo to entry room

When the igloo is ready, Kenalogak gathers twigs for a fire to make tea. But she does not go far to dig under the snow for the twigs. The land is covered by low clouds, and if she wanders too far, she will not be able to see the igloo and might lose her way. But someday, like her father, she will be able to tell direction by observing the *sastrugi*, wind patterns in the snow. Her father can always find his way home, even when he travels far with his sled and dogs.

Grandmother and Grandfather have invited a friend, who's a good drummer, to join a celebration in the new igloo. After feasting on raw frozen fish, the drummer begins *Kaylauzak*, playing his drum while singing and dancing. Kaylauzak is often performed to thank the life spirit for helping the Inuit catch many fish or bring home many tuktu. And sometimes the drum dance is simply performed to celebrate how good life is.

After the drum dance, Grandmother and her friend play a singing game called *Kayavak*. Whispering from deep in their throats into a pot, they mimic each other's words and sounds while singing faster and faster. As the two friends play, they create a beautiful soft echo, like the sounds of the wind laughing and sighing outside the igloo.

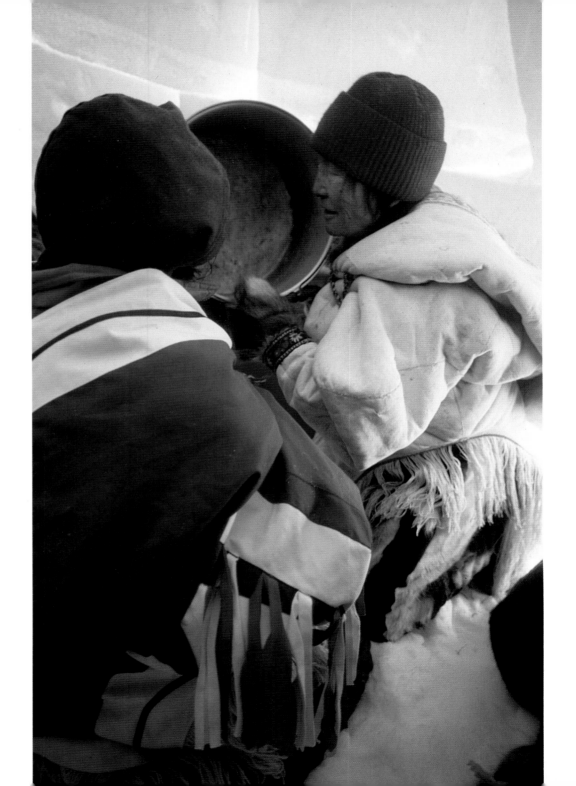

The next day when the winds are calm, Kenalogak fishes on the ice. She is proud to learn the ways of the Inuit, ways that respect the spirit of life in a land of snow and ice.

Winds up to forty miles per hour blew the snow like spray off the sea all night long. In the morning, I discovered that a drift had covered the opening of my igloo, sealing me inside. I felt like a snail with my shell of snow blocks winding around me.

I had slept in the igloo built for Kenalogak's grandparents for Kaylauzak, drum dancing, and Kayavak, throat singing. I wanted to savor the sense of celebration that remained behind. Although drum dancing can be a simple celebration giving thanks for everyday life, including success in the hunt, the meditative quality of the dance and the song also honors the continual flow of life through all that exists in the world. The airy, guttural throat singing, a haunting, whispering wind in the domed igloo, is another form of meditation.

After digging out of the igloo, all I could see was white above, below, and beside me. Engulfed in this whiteout, I had no sense of direction, yet I had to make my way to Kenalogak's family's village on the shores of Qamanituaq, also known as Baker Lake.

Kenalogak's father, Utak, had shown me how to observe and interpret the hardened ridges of snow, called sastrugi, that mark the direction of the wind; he is able to judge his direction of travel in relation to these ridges. I knew the approximate angle I had crossed the sastrugi when I skied to my igloo after leaving Utak and his family the evening before. Now I would have to try and angle back the same way, and given the distance I had to cover, a small mistake in judgment would take me a great deal off course.

I reached the village, but not at the site I intended; if I had had a longer distance to travel, I surely would have missed the village entirely and skied out into the vast, frozen expanse. What did it matter that I had climbed Himalayan peaks in the winter season? This was the Barren Lands, known for being consistently the coldest place on earth. When I came in the door of my friends' small home, Utak laughed and said, "So, you survived."

Kenalogak's family lives in a village that has no roads or power lines leading to it. Yet the people who live here have modern homes with electricity because oil for the village generator is brought into the bay by barge once a year when the ice melts. The barge also brings groceries to stock the large local store. Although Kenalogak's parents now live in a modern house, they both spent their childhoods in igloos. And today, when hunting the caribou that continue to migrate across the land, the people from Qamanituaq still build igloos from snow and ice for shelter.

Although the Coastal Inuit depended on seals, whales, and other sea life, Kenalogak's people traditionally lived inland and were dependent on tuktu, the caribou, for survival. They traveled in family groups, and except for the respect given to the shamans or wise men considered powerful because of the visions they received from the spirit world, there was no political hierarchy. But with the arrival of European fur traders came widespread social, economic, political, and environmental changes. Also with the Qablunat, or white men, came rifles.

The pelts of the fur-bearing animals found in the arctic were extremely popular with Qablunat. Wide-scale trapping decimated the caribou. Large numbers of caribou were killed to use as bait for traplines. Others swallowed poisons that were set out to kill the arctic fox and other valuable fur-bearing animals. The great herds of caribou began to dwindle and change their migratory routes. Soon, ignoring their traditional lives, the once independent Inuit hunters became dependent trappers, bartering furs with Qablunat for new needs such as rifles, ammunition, flour, sugar, tobacco, and tea.

The introduction of foreigners and their ways changed the lives of the Inuit, who had looked at hunting as a contract between two partners: the life-giving animal and the reverent hunter. The traditional Inuit hunters had respect for the life spirit flowing through all natural things.

Because the tuktu gave its life so the Inuit could survive, the hunter honored this great sacrifice by utilizing all parts of the animal. Skins were used for clothing, bedding, and bags; bones and antlers were made into tools and weapons; and sinew was used for lashing and making thread for sewing. Nothing was wasted, even the meat not needed immediately was stored or cached in the snow to dry for later use. The Inuit basically eat only meat and fat. At first I wondered how they could survive on such a singular diet. But I was surprised to learn that a diet of meat balanced by about forty percent fat provides everything human metabolism requires.

One evening Kenalogak's mother, Akak, told me a story about her childhood, when she lived on the land with her grandparents. She recalled the time when the caribou herds that had fed the Inuit for thousands of years started disappearing. Not even the inuksuk, the rock men, were driving the caribou to the Inuit to hunt, and the people were starving. Akak and her grandparents, along with other family members, stayed on the ice until it began to melt in the spring and puddles of water formed on its surface. This signaled the time for the Inuit to move to the shore and build new shelters. That year everyone was thin and weak: one man couldn't even walk to the shore; he died on the ice. Fortunately, her uncle killed a lone caribou he found crossing a river, and he cut off a hindquarter for her family. She remembered how good the raw meat tasted. Until her uncle had killed the caribou, she had been eating the skin of her fur parka, which was all she had to keep herself warm.

The Canadian government transported the starving Inuit to designated areas. Akak and her sister were flown to Qamanituaq, and the rest of their family came later by dogsled. In the beginning at Qamanituaq, the people still lived in igloos. Then schools were built, and the children were taught to speak English and were given English names. But Kenalogak's father, Utak, said all he could think about while sitting in a classroom was "hunting, hunting, hunting." For Utak, school had been learning from his family the traditional skills needed to live off the land. The people placed at Qamanituaq by the Canadian government were separated from their land and suffered a sense of dislocation. Now, many years later, Kenalogak is learning her Inuit culture and language in school, and sometimes she and her friends even use their Inuit names in class.

As I skied away from the igloo, wrapped in a white cloud, I remembered the sounds, sights, and feelings of Kaylauzak and Kayavak. I thought about the changes brought to this area of the world by Qablunat, altering the rhythms of the lives of the Inuit and their connection to the land. What had happened to the Inuit's right to their land, to make their own choices? I later learned the Canadian government granted about half of the Northwest Territories to the Inuit. This area will be called Nunavut, meaning "our land," to be governed by the Inuit themselves. I hope for Kenalogak and her family that it will be enough.

—*Jan Reynolds*

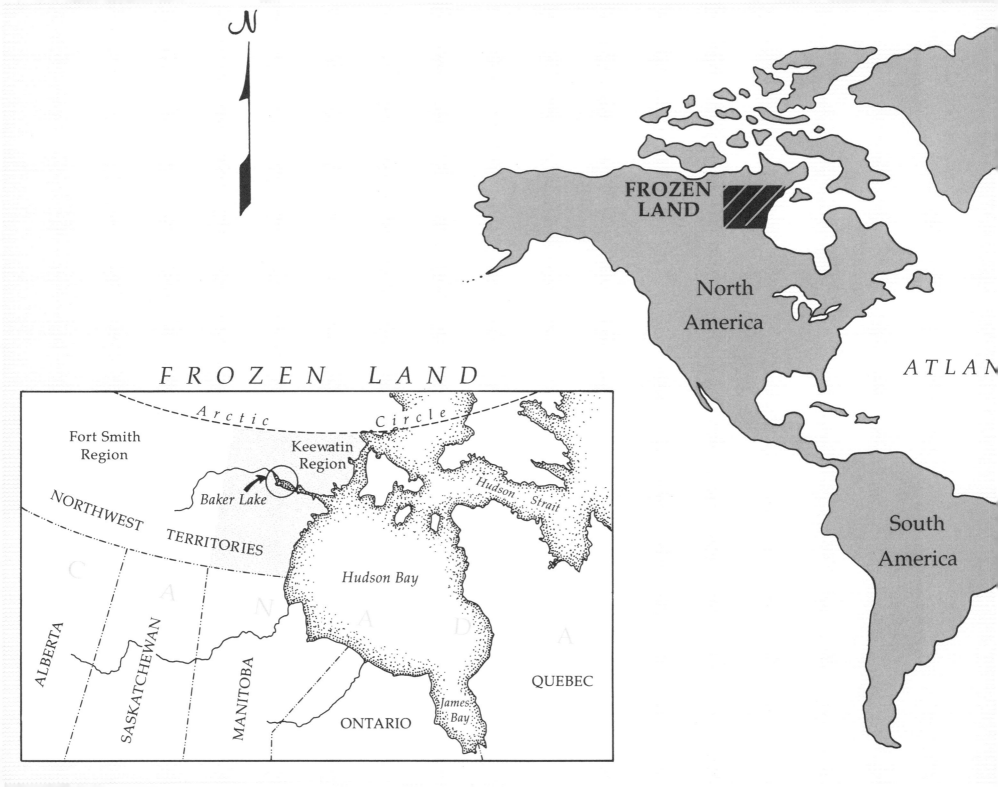

N

FROZEN
LAND

North
America

ATLAN

South
America

FROZEN LAND

Arctic Circle

Fort Smith
Region

Keewatin
Region

Baker Lake

Hudson Strait

NORTHWEST

TERRITORIES

Hudson Bay

ALBERTA

SASKATCHEWAN

MANITOBA

QUEBEC

James
Bay

ONTARIO

C A N A D A

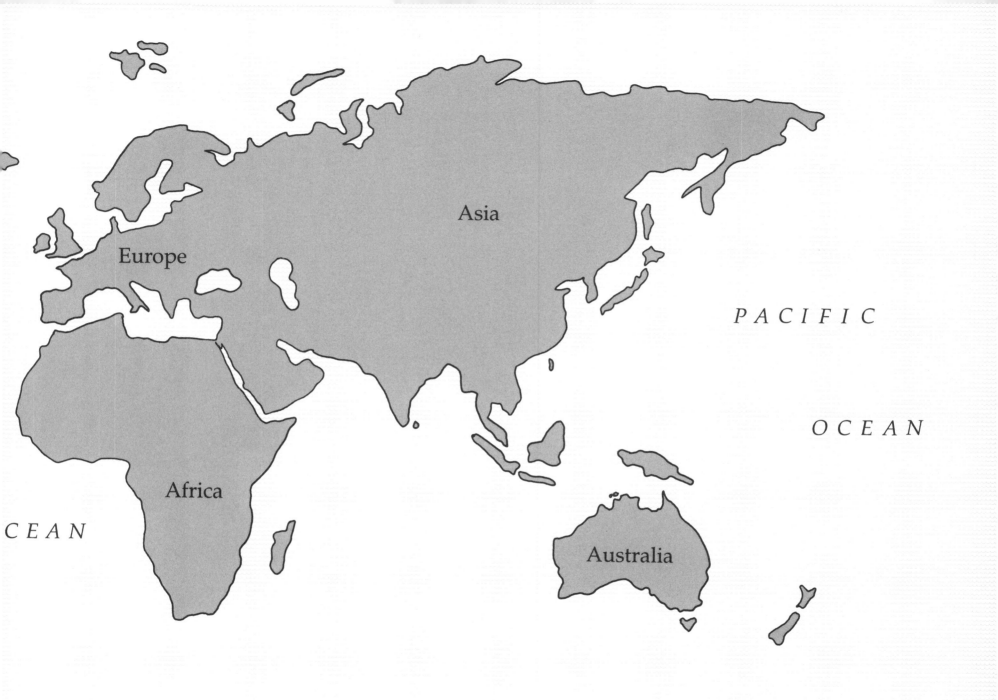

Europe

Asia

PACIFIC

OCEAN

Africa

CEAN

Australia